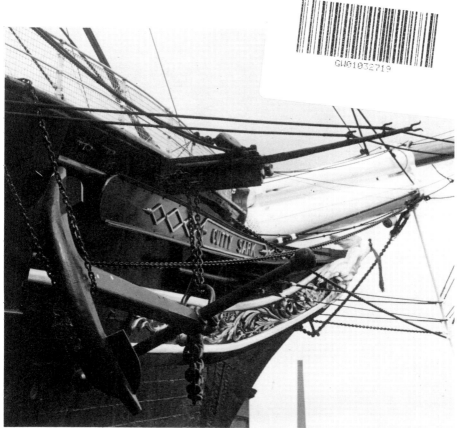

ABOVE: *The starboard bower anchor of the 'Cutty Sark' at Greenwich. The photograph shows the cathead, the shank painter and the studlink anchor cable. This anchor is a wooden replica, but the ship's port anchor, which rests on the bottom of the dry dock, is original.*

COVER: *The Anchor Wharf at the National Maritime Museum, Greenwich.*

ANCHORS

N. E. Upham

Shire Publications Ltd

CONTENTS

Set in 9 on 9 point Times roman and printed in Great Britain by C. I. Thomas & Sons (Haverfordwest) Ltd, Press Buildings, Merlins Bridge, Haverfordwest.

ACKNOWLEDGEMENTS

With the exceptions given below the illustrations used in this book are from the collection of the National Maritime Museum and the author wishes to thank the Trustees and Director of the museum for permission to reproduce them. The line drawings are by David J. Eveleigh and other illustrations are acknowledged as follows: Cadbury Lamb, page 3; Honor Frost and the Editor, *Mariners' Mirror*, page 4 (top two drawings); British Museum, page 5; Dorset Natural History and Archaeological Society and Dorset County Museum, page 9 (lower); Carl V. Solver and the *Mariners' Mirror*, page 10; Colin Martin, page 12; the City Engineer, Portsmouth, page 31 (top).

Negative numbers of the illustrations from the collection of the National Maritime Museum are as follows: page 1, C6665; page 4 (lower), C5459/31 and C5459/34 (photographs by the author); page 7, C7054 and C7053; page 9 (top), C6754/20; page 11, C6754/15, B4900 and B4919; page 13, C6997/a; page 14, C6996/a; page 15, C6998/a and C6998/b; page 16, A77; page 18, C7051 and C6755/2; page 19, C4564/a; page 20, C6995 and C6994; page 21, C6963 and C6993; page 22, C6755/7; page 23, C6756/3 and C6757/8; page 24, C7063; page 27, C4076/3; page 29 (top), C7047; page 31 (bottom), unnumbered, from the museum's Historic Photographs Collection. The cover photograph is also reproduced by courtesy of the Trustees of the National Maritime Museum.

The author gives special thanks to Miss Fredericka Smith, who gave great assistance in the preparation of the text.

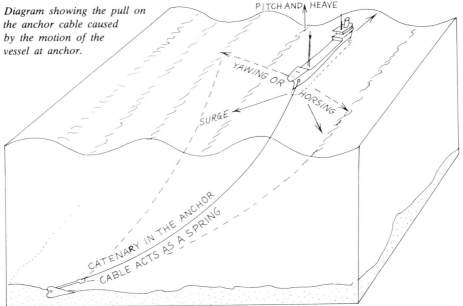

Diagram showing the pull on the anchor cable caused by the motion of the vessel at anchor.

PITCH AND HEAVE

YAWING OR HORSING

SURGE

CATENARY IN THE ANCHOR CABLE ACTS AS A SPRING

Replica sheet and starboard bower anchors, HMS 'Victory', Portsmouth Dockyard. The shank painter, which confines the shank of the anchor to the ship's side and prevents the flukes flying off the billboard, is situated to the right of the upper anchor fluke.

INTRODUCTION

Ever since craft propelled by paddle, oar or sail have been capable of making an offing from a riverbank, lakeside or seashore the occupants have found it necessary to hold the vessel in a fixed position by attaching it to the bottom when in shallow water. This might be to avoid an adverse drift in a tideway or current, to hold a vessel in a sheltered anchorage when working cargo, or to prevent it from being wrecked on a lee shore.

This book is a brief survey of the evolution of the anchor. It would appear that this development was empirical. Some nineteenth-century anchor designs were claimed to be based on scientific theory but it is difficult to substantiate this. Improved manufacturing processes are more likely to have influenced anchor performance. The Admiralty and the United States Navy pioneered scientific investigation into the design of high holding power anchors during the mid twentieth century.

The first anchors were simply weights attached to the craft by rope made from natural fibres. These stone anchors held by friction and were inefficient. Mariners soon realised that it was not the weight of the anchor that was significant but its proclivity to embed and the resulting holding power. By enclosing the stone in a wooden frame with projecting teeth, as shown in Chinese anchors and other killicks, an additional ploughing action was achieved which greatly improved the holding power.

A long scope or length of cable also increased the efficiency of the killick or anchor. Experience proved that a length of cable more than three and a half to five times the depth of water in which the craft was anchored should be used, the depth of water being the governing factor, though anchor weight or type does affect the length of cable necessary to hold a vessel securely. In a gale, extra cable veered out on a single anchor is often more effective than letting go additional anchors if only a short scope of cable is used.

The principal parts of an anchor are: the vertical stem or *shank;* the arms terminating in the blades or *flukes;* and the cross bar or *stock,* which turns the anchor into an attitude that enables it to dig in. In modern stockless anchors this is achieved by tripping palms on the head or *crown.*

Since the 1960s the vast size of container ships and even larger dry and liquid bulk carriers, some in excess of 500,000 tonnes deadweight, has focused attention on the special design requirements of anchors and ground tackle.

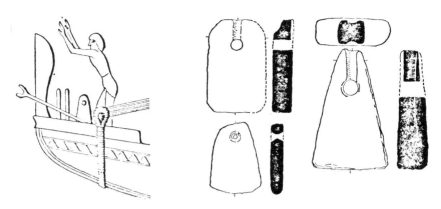

ABOVE LEFT: *An Egyptian stone anchor standing on the prow of a boat. From a bas-relief in the tomb of king Sahu-re at Abusir, about 3000 BC.*

ABOVE RIGHT: *Hammer-dressed limestone anchors, Phoenician, about 1900 BC.*

BELOW LEFT: *A stone anchor found during the construction of Raysut harbour, Oman, 1976. It measures 66 inches (1680 mm) long and is 9½ inches (240 mm) in diameter at the top and 14½ inches (370 mm) at its lower end. The teeth are missing.*

BELOW RIGHT: *A stone anchor found at Raysut harbour, 1976, measuring 50 inches (1270 mm) long by 39 inches (1000 mm) wide. The stone is about 8¼ inches (210 mm) thick. Similar composite anchors attributed to the Greeks and dated to the fourth century BC have been found in the Mediterranean.*

4

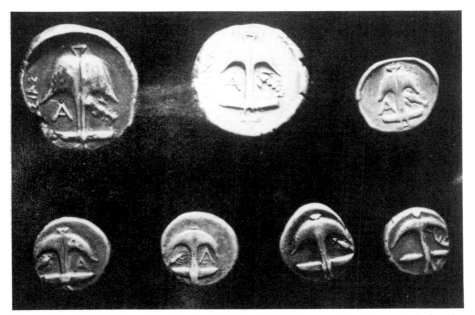

Greek coins of c 400 BC, attributed to Apollonia Pontica in Thrace and depicting a stocked anchor with a ring for the anchor buoy rope on the crown.

FROM ANCIENT TIMES TO THE MIDDLE AGES

Egyptian anchors about 2600 BC were shaped stones with horizontal holes bored through to take rope cable and sticks. Anchors of this type are illustrated in a Fifth Dynasty bas-relief from the tomb of Sahu-re, *c* 3000 BC, at Abusir.

A Phoenician anchor of *c* 1900 BC, from the Temple of Obelisks at Byblos, Lebanon, is shaped from limestone dressed by hammer. This type was adapted to anchor on a sandy bottom and is still used by Turkish fishermen today. Stone anchors of a similar shape, though probably from a later period, were found at Raysut, Oman, during harbour construction about 1978.

The Chinese emperor Yu (2205-2197 BC), a patron of engineering works, is an early claimant to have invented the killick, or wood and stone anchor. In western civilisation the word for an anchor first appears in the Greek language, meaning curved or hooked, the Latin word *anchora* meaning bent. Stra-bo (64 BC to AD 25) writes in his *Geography* of inventions reported by Ephorus (*c* 400-340 BC) and attributes the anchor with arms to Anacharsis (*fl* 590 BC).

A Greek gem of *c* 500 BC, found in Sardinia, depicts a shipwright shaping an anchor, surrounded by a chain cable. Some Greek anchors had wooden shanks and arms. A lead insert in the stock and arms gave the necessary weight to ensure that the anchor took up a position from which it could dig into the seabed. Iron tips on the bills of the anchor's arms assisted the digging in.

Some Greek anchors were made from iron. Those used by the Athenian navy seem to have been under 56 pounds (25 kg) in weight. To increase the weight, the lower part of the shank had stones or lead attached by clamps. The anchor cable was usually made from rope, though chain cable was sometimes used nearest the anchor, where the cable lay on the seabed and was likely to chafe against rocks. The rope cables are recorded as being between 4½ and 6 inches (114-152 mm) in circumference. Four cables of each size were carried and these doubled as shore moorings when necessary.

Early representations of Greek anchors with arms and a stock appear on coins attributed to Apollonia Pontica (Thrace), *c* 400 BC. These anchors have a ring for the anchor buoy rope on their crowns.

The importance of the anchor as a means of saving a vessel caught on a lee shore is indicated by the number of anchors carried in ships immediately before and at the commencement of the Roman period. Off the island of Giannutri, three iron and four wooden anchors with lead stocks were found near a mid second-century BC wreck. A wreck near Taranto, *c* AD 100, had five anchors, each weighing 12 hundredweight (600 kg).

Near Yassi Ada, in a shipwreck dated *c* AD 625, the vessel having a length of 62 feet (18.9 m) and a 16 foot (4.87 m) beam, two anchor stocks and eleven anchors were found. Six of these anchors weighed 1.43 hundredweight (73.5 kg) each, three about 2.6 hundredweight (129 kg) each, and the other two were of intermediate weight. The approximate weight of the stocks was 32 pounds (14.5 kg) and 69 pounds (31.4 kg). The total weight of the vessel's anchors was about 1.26 tons (1279 kg).

According to Herodotus King Hiero's ship was equipped with eight iron and four wooden anchors, but the best known reference to anchors in the ancient world is the account of St Paul's shipwreck (Acts of the Apostles, chapter 27, verses 28-30). This account indicates that St Paul's ship had at least six and possibly eight anchors.

ROMAN ANCHORS

The recovery of two Roman anchors from Lake Nemi in Italy between 1929 and 1931, when the lake was drained, provided a great deal of information on the types of anchors used aboard Roman vessels at the beginning of the Christian era. The anchors found belonged to a ship or state barge built during the reign

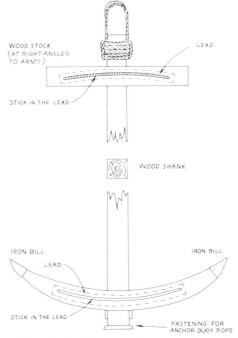

Although the Greeks used iron anchors of under 51 pounds (23.3 kg), many were made of wood with lead inserts in the arms and stocks to give weight and to ensure that the anchor would take up the correct attitude to dig into the seabed. Iron tips were fitted to the bills to reinforce them.

of the emperor Caligula, *c* AD 40. One of the anchors was made from wood and was fitted with a lead stock. This confirmed that numerous lead bars with square holes in the centre previously recovered from the Mediterranean Sea were anchor stocks and not the arms of anchors as some authorities had suggested. The wooden anchor was found in a correct holding attitude, with one arm dug in and the stock parallel to the ground. A thick rope anchor cable was attached to the anchor ring, the circumference of which was 18¾ inches (476 mm).

The second anchor discovered was made from iron and sheathed in wood. The wood gave the iron core a larger bearing surface and an advantage in thick mud as found on the bottom of Lake Nemi. The extra area of the shank and arms prevented the anchor sinking too far

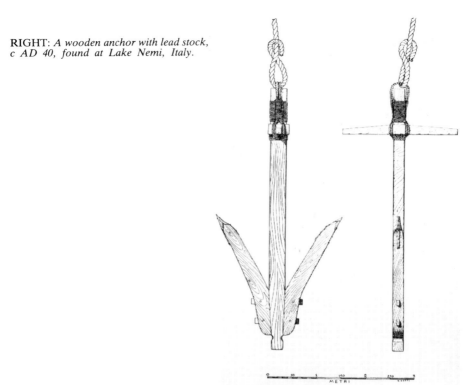

RIGHT: *A wooden anchor with lead stock, c AD 40, found at Lake Nemi, Italy.*

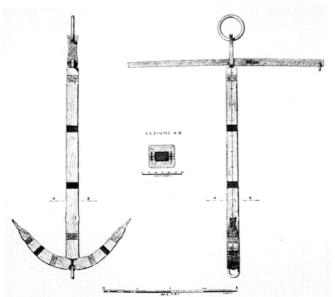

LEFT: *An iron anchor sheathed in wood, c AD 40, found at Lake Nemi, Italy.*

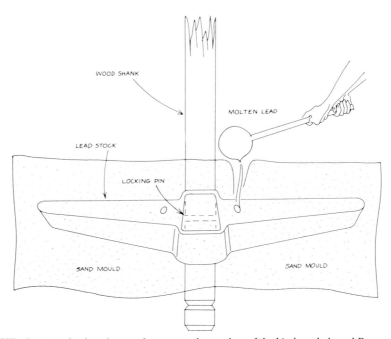

ABOVE: *Casting a lead anchor stock on a wooden anchor of the kind used aboard Roman vessels.*

BELOW: *Method of filling a wooden anchor stock with lead and casting the lead bridge piece to strengthen the arms.*

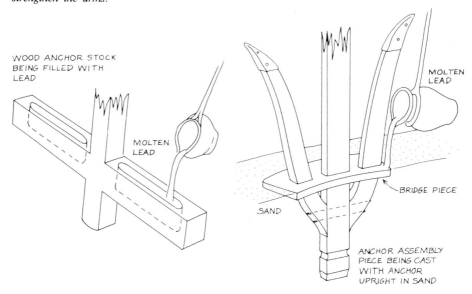

A Roman lead anchor stock, weighing 103 pounds (46.2 kg), with a lead filling piece, recovered from the Mediterranean and now in the National Maritime Museum collection.

into the mud and facilitated the weighing of the anchor. The iron stock was held in position with a forelock and cotter pin, similar to those reintroduced in the nineteenth century. A ring was situated in the crown of the anchor for attachment of the anchor buoy line. The marking of the position of the anchor was necessary in order that this valuable item of ship's equipment might be located if slipped in an emergency. The weight of the anchor was stamped on one of the arms as 1275 Roman pounds (approximately 913 imperial pounds or 414 kg).

The lead anchor stock was made by being cast on to the shank, which was upended in the sand mould. A hole was drilled or burnt through the shank at the position the stock was required. As the stock was cast, the lead flowed through the hole, forming a locking pin to hold the stock in position.

The Veneti, a tribe of southern Brittany who later settled in Wessex, were reported by Julius Caesar as having anchors secured fast by iron chain or rope cables. This anchor and its chain cable were found at Bulbury Camp, a hillfort of the Veneti near Bere Regis, Dorset.

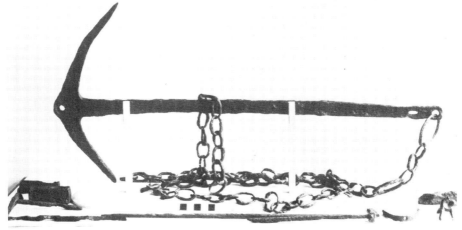

9

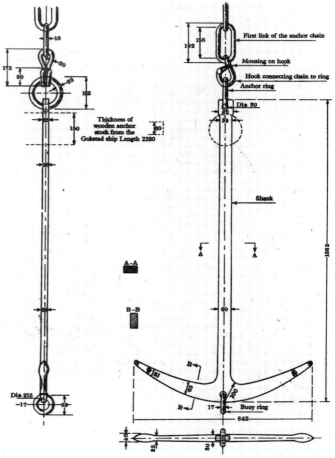

Drawing of the anchor found in the Viking ship at Ladby, Denmark. The anchor stock was not recovered but is assumed to have been a tapered wooden stock similar to that found with the Gotstad ship.

In 1974 a lead anchor stock was found in the sea off the Welsh coast near Aberdarewllyn, Gwynedd. Now in the collection of the National Museum of Wales at Cardiff, it is the only anchor of this type to be recovered from British waters and weighs 158 pounds (71.5 kg) and is 3 feet 10 inches (1.18 m) long.

The Veneti tribe in southern Brittany was said by Julius Caesar to have had anchors secured fast by iron chains instead of rope fibre cables. In 1881 an anchor with a chain cable was discovered in the Veneti hillfort of Bulbury Camp, Bere Regis, Dorset. This important find is now in the Dorset County Museum at Dorchester.

DANISH ANCHORS

Another early anchor of great interest was found with a Danish ship of *c* AD 950 at Ladby on the island of Fyn, Denmark. This anchor no longer has its wooden stock but was found with some 30 feet (9.14 m) of chain cable attached. A windlass operated by hand spikes was provided on board the Ladby ship for use in hoisting the yard on which the sail was set and to weigh the anchor.

KILLICKS

Small anchors made from wood, stones and rope lashings have traditionally been used by the fishermen and seamen of north-west Europe, the Mediterranean, the Red Sea, the Americas, India, China and the Far East. They are called *killicks*. The wooden arms and stocks are of hardwood or willow. In some cases the stocks are fitted to the crown of the anchor, a feature of the modern Darnforth anchor. The stone attached to the anchor near the crown gave the flukes the right attitude to embed when the weight of the craft came on the anchor cable. To weigh the killick, the craft was pulled ahead on the cable until directly over it. It was then quite easy to break the killick out of the ground and haul it on board.

MEDIEVAL ANCHORS

Little is known of medieval anchors as no examples have survived from this period. Some evidence, however, comes from illustrations of anchors in the Bayeux Tapestry, on wax seals and in religious illuminated works. The late thirteenth-century seal of Portsmouth clearly shows an anchor with the ring provided for the anchor buoy line. The increased size of ships resulted in the introduction of the hawse hole. Larger

ABOVE: *A Canadian killick in the collection of the National Maritime Museum.*

BELOW LEFT: *The second seal of the town of Portsmouth, thirteenth century. The anchor of the vessel is prominent and the ring for the anchor buoy rope can be clearly seen.*

BELOW RIGHT: *Early fourteenth-century seal of Winchelsea, East Sussex. This is the earliest known representation of a windlass. The two seamen at the after end are hauling on the hand spikes in the windlass barrel. The arrangement is similar to that on the Ladby ship found in Denmark.*

anchors had heavier members and so careful welding was necessary, and eventually water-powered trip hammers were used in the welding processes.

The iron for medieval anchors came from Sussex or northern Spain, Spanish iron being shipped in vessels carrying pilgrims from the shrine of St James of Compostella, via the port of Corunna.

Statutes regulated the number of anchors and cables to be carried. In some cases as many as fifteen anchors were required, but some of these must have been quite small.

THE SIXTEENTH, SEVENTEENTH AND EIGHTEENTH CENTURIES

In modern times divers have recovered anchors from the wrecks of Spanish, vessels such as *La Trinidad Valencera* (Balanzora). A Venetian merchantman, she was one of the largest vessels in the Duke of Medina Sidonia's Armada fleet of 1588 and was wrecked off Donegal. The anchor found on the wreck site could have had a pronounced bill or pea at the apex of the triangular palm. One of the anchors has lost an arm because of the failure of the weld at the point where it joins the shank. The anchors are thought to be of Spanish or Venetian origin.

The earliest contemporary drawing of an anchor with details of its weight and dimensions appears in *Fragments of Ancient Shipwrightry*, attributed to Matthew Baker, dating from the late sixteenth or early seventeenth century.

Most anchors of the sixteenth and seventeenth centuries had curved arms, but as larger anchors were required the straight-arm anchor was introduced in English vessels. The flukes were generally the shape of equilateral triangles and half the length of the arms. The anchor ring was of a slightly smaller diameter than the fluke. Mainwaring's *Seamen's Directory* (1622) states that the shank is twice as long as one of the flukes, plus half the beam. The beam was probably the distance between the two bills or tops of the flukes. The anchor stock was roughly the same length as the shank. It was made from timbers bound with iron hoops which had been driven on when heated, then shrunk on to hold the two halves of the stock together. Wooden pegs called treenails were used to secure the timbers in the stock, which was straight on the top and tapered on the other three sides.

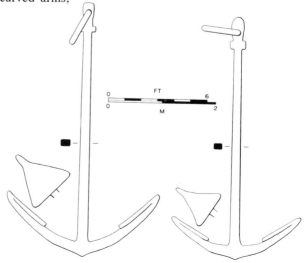

Drawing of the two anchors from 'La Trinidad Valencera', wrecked in Kinnagoe Bay, Ireland, in 1588.

12

In the next Place I fhall fhew the particular Shape and Dimenfions of the Anchors, obferving that it's general, for the length of the Shank of the biggeft Anchor, in any Ship, to be $\frac{2}{5}$ of the Ships extream breadth.

Tunnage of the Six Sizes —·—	1677 Tuns		1488 Tuns		969 Tuns		625 Tuns		364 Tuns		225 Tuns	
	C. qr. l.		C. qr. l.		C. qr. l.		C. qr. l.		C. qr. l.		C. qr. l.	
Weight of the biggeft Anchor —	71 : 2 : 0		54 : 0 : 0		45 : 0 : 0		30 : 0 : 0		18 : 3 : 6		11 : 2 : 1	
Cube Root of the Weight - —	$4-\frac{2}{10}$		4		$3-\frac{5}{10}$		$3-\frac{1}{10}$		$2-\frac{66}{100}$		$2-\frac{26}{100}$	
	feet	Inch.	feet	Inch.	feet	Inch.	feet	Inch.	feet	Inch	feet	Inch.
Length of the Shank as aforefaid·	18	6	18	2	16	1	14	4	12	2	10	8
Bignefs of the great End of ditto·	0	$11\frac{1}{2}$	0	$11\frac{1}{10}$	0	$10\frac{1}{10}$	0	$8\frac{8}{10}$	0	$7\frac{3}{10}$	0	$6\frac{14}{10}$
Ditto at the fmall end ·	0	$8\frac{11}{10}$	0	$8\frac{7}{10}$	0	$7\frac{7}{10}$	0	$6\frac{7}{10}$	0	$5\frac{5}{10}$	0	$4\frac{7}{10}$
Length of the Square —·—	2	11	2	$10\frac{7}{10}$	2	$6\frac{4}{10}$	2	3	1	11	1	8
Length to the Nut —	1	11	1	$10\frac{5}{10}$	1	$8\frac{7}{10}$	1	$5\frac{6}{10}$	1	$3\frac{1}{10}$	1	$1\frac{4}{10}$
Bignefs of the Nut Square ·—	0	$2\frac{7}{10}$	0	$2\frac{16}{10}$	0	2	0	$1\frac{76}{10}$	0	$1\frac{51}{10}$	0	$1\frac{14}{10}$
Diamiter of the Rings infide clear·	2	$1\frac{1}{4}$	2	1	1	10	1	$7\frac{6}{10}$	1	3	1	2
Bignefs of the Ring —·—	0	4	0	$3\frac{24}{10}$	0	$3\frac{48}{10}$	0	$3\frac{6}{10}$	0	3	0	3
Diameter of the Hole for the Ring	0	$4\frac{6}{10}$	0	$4\frac{5}{10}$	0	$3\frac{8}{10}$	0	$3\frac{4}{10}$	0	3	0	$2\frac{66}{10}$
Length of the Crown ——	1	2	1	$1\frac{7}{10}$	0	$11\frac{7}{10}$	0	$9\frac{4}{10}$	0	$8\frac{7}{10}$	0	$7\frac{2}{10}$
Length of the Arm ———	7	0	6	9	6	1	5	1	4	$0\frac{7}{10}$	4	$0\frac{4}{10}$
Breadth of the Flook ——·—	2	8	2	$7\frac{5}{10}$	2	$3\frac{8}{10}$	2	$0\frac{4}{10}$	1	9	1	6
Length of ditto ———	3	9	3	$8\frac{1}{2}$	3	$3\frac{2}{10}$	2	$10\frac{4}{10}$	2	$5\frac{5}{10}$	2	2
Thicknefs of ditto——	0	$2\frac{2}{10}$	0	$2\frac{5}{10}$	0	$2\frac{51}{10}$	0	$2\frac{1}{10}$	0	$1\frac{2}{10}$	0	$1\frac{68}{10}$
Square of the Arm at the Flook—	0	7	0	$6\frac{2}{10}$	0	$6\frac{1}{10}$	0	$5\frac{2}{10}$	0	$4\frac{5}{10}$	0	$4\frac{2}{10}$
Length of the Bill ———	0	$10\frac{1}{4}$	0	$10\frac{3}{10}$	0	$9\frac{1}{10}$	0	8	0	$6\frac{2}{10}$	0	$6\frac{1}{10}$
Rounding of the Flook ·——	0	$1\frac{16}{10}$	0	$1\frac{14}{10}$	0	$1\frac{1}{10}$	0	$0\frac{89}{10}$	0	$0\frac{26}{10}$	0	$0\frac{66}{10}$
Clutching of the Arm ———	3	6	3	$5\frac{1}{3}$	3	$0\frac{4}{10}$	2	6	2	$4\frac{1}{2}$	2	$1\frac{2}{10}$
Infide meeting ·— —·—	6	6										
Outfide meeting — ——·—	6	6										
Middle meeting ———·—	6	6										

A table of anchor dimensions for the Royal Navy, from William Sutherland's 'Britain's Glory or Shipbuilding Unvailed' (1711), the first comprehensive English book on naval architecture.

SEVENTEENTH-CENTURY ANCHORS

Captain John Smith published *A Sea Grammar* in 1627, giving lists of the types of anchors carried by ships of that period. The *kedger* was the smallest of the anchors, used in calm weather or in a weak tidal stream. Working a ship up or down river with the tide was known as kedging. These anchors could be used in one of the ship's boats or for heaving the ship's head about the cable. The *stream* anchor was only a little larger than the kedger (or kedge) and used to stem an easy stream or tide. The *bow* anchors numbered four in all, the strongest being the *sheet* anchor, used in times of emergency. Anchor weight was in proportion to the size of the ship. A ship of 500 tons burthen would have a sheet anchor of 2000 pounds (907 kg). The largest anchors carried were 3500 pounds (1588 kg).

The sheet or best anchor was carried on the starboard side as the wind in the northern hemisphere shifts from south-west to north-west on the passage of a depression over a ship at anchor. First the port *bower* anchor would be let go. As the wind increased, the starboard bower or sheet anchor with both cables was paid out until the vessel was held. When the wind veered both cables would lie out ahead of the ship. Had the reverse procedure with the anchors been adopted the cables would have crossed when the wind shifted to the north-west. In the southern hemisphere the reverse is true: the starboard anchor is let go first as the wind shifts to the left on the passage of a depression. The strongest winds usually occur after the shift of wind as the barometer rises, hence the old saying 'Fast rise after fall brings the strongest blow of all'.

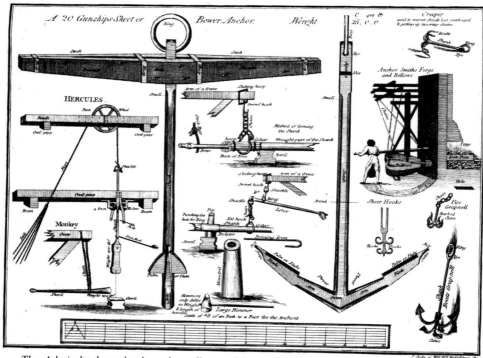

The Admiralty long-shank anchor, illustrated in Steel's 'Elements of Seamanship' (1794).

ANCHORS IN THE EIGHTEENTH CENTURY

An account of anchors, their dimensions and the forging techniques used to produce them appears in William Sutherland's *Britain's Glory or Shipbuilding Unvailed* (1717). Sutherland writes that Royal Navy regulations stipulated that the length of the shank of the largest anchor on a naval vessel was two fifths of the vessel's extreme breadth. The Admiralty issued lists of the dimensions fixed for each rate of Royal Navy ships. These lists were called the Establishment.

Eighteenth-century anchors were made from a number of iron rods or bars, which were tied together, heated and then forged under a trip hammer into one bar to form the shank or arms. These component parts were then welded together. At this time there were no methods of checking welds and hidden defects often remained undetected. Anchor arms frequently broke off when under severe strain. *A Treatise on Anchors,* published by Richard Pering in 1819, records that naval dockyards had large numbers of anchors awaiting repair.

WEIGHING ANCHOR IN A SHIP OF THE LINE

The anchor cable of a 74-gun ship of the line was about 18 inches (457 mm) in circumference and was therefore too heavy and unmanageable to take to a capstan. In order to heave on the cable and thus weigh the anchor, a smaller endless rope, termed a *messenger,* was taken around the capstan, then led forward via rollers situated under the deckhead of the upper deck. Near the hawse holes the messenger was passed around a vertical roller, then led back aft to the capstan.

RIGHT: *A bundle of bars or rods for an anchor, fastened together by iron brackets and ready for the furnace. The process begins with the welding and forging of the smaller end of the shank and includes alternately swinging from furnace to hammer and back for heating and welding.*

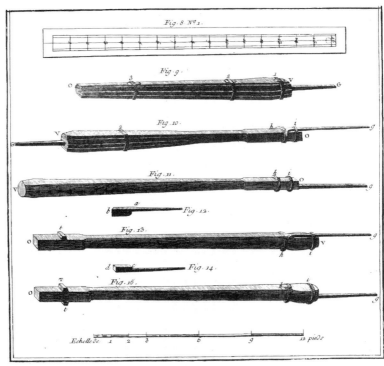

BELOW: *The anchor forge, showing the shank half welded. The claw is fastened to the square-shaped end marked O. The thick end V is heated so that the rudder VG may be cut off.*

15

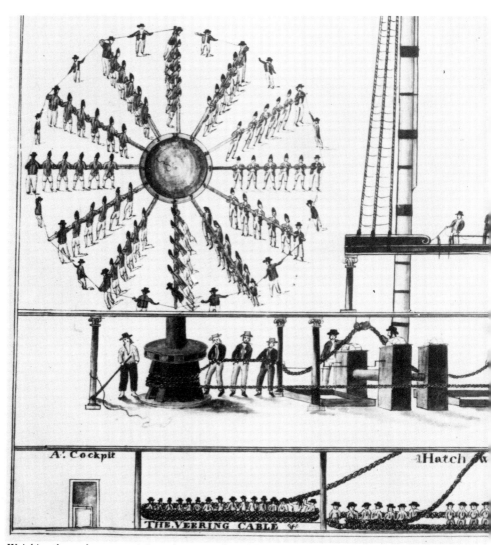

Weighing the anchor on an eighteenth-century ship of the line. Middle right, on the fo'c'slehead may be seen the cat davit and the fish davit. On the main deck below are the capstan drum, cable and messenger. The forward capstan is termed the jeer capstan, and the cable bitts are situated between the forward hatch and the seaman passing the nipper. In the hold are the seamen stowing the wet and

To weigh the anchor, short light lines called *nippers* were passed around both cable and messenger, binding them together. This was done by an able seaman, who then passed the nipper over to a boy rating, who walked along with the cable as it was hove in, holding the end of the nipper, until he reached the hatchway, down which the cable passed to the cable tier in the hold. Having removed the nipper at the hatchway, the boy then ran forward with it to the

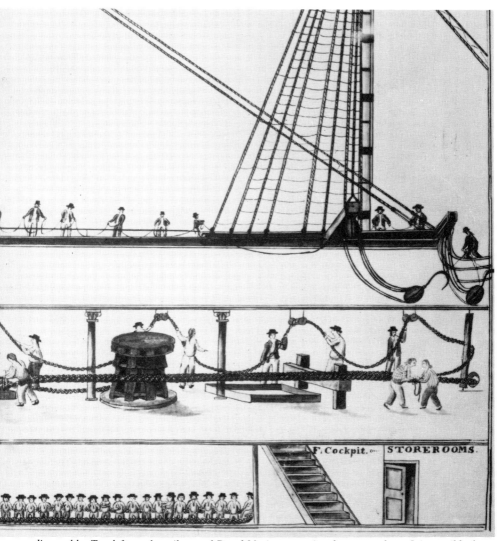

slimy cable. Top left are the sailors and Royal Marines manning the capstan bars. It is possible that they may have had to heave in 90 fathoms (165 metres) or more of cable to weigh the anchor, which was a slow and tedious job, often carried out to the singing of sea shanties and the accompaniment of a fiddle.

seaman so that it could be used again to marry the cable to the messenger.

To make the cable fast to the cable or riding bitts, the cable was 'stoppered off' by a series of rope stoppers attached to ringbolts on the deck between the man-ger (formed by a short bulkhead situated abaft the hawse holes) and the cable bitts. When the cable was turned up the stoppers could be removed, and the vessel would be riding on her cable secured to the cable bitts.

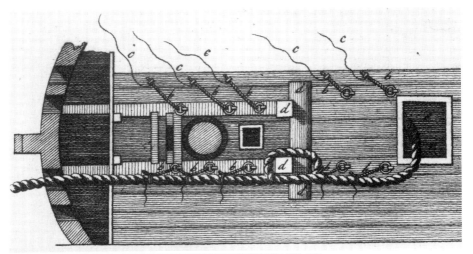

ABOVE: *Cable stoppers.*

LEFT: *An Admiralty long-shank anchor of c 1750, recovered off Sheerness. The wooden stock is filled with nails to protect it from attack by teredo worm. It may have been the bower anchor of a forty-four gun ship. It is now displayed on the Anchor Wharf of the National Maritime Museum.*

A contemporary model of a seventy gun ship of c 1740, illustrating the Admiralty long-shank anchor with the serving on the anchor ring, the anchor buoy and the fish davit, a portable beam which could be transferred from one side of the fo'c'slehead to the other. Note also the cathead with its tackle used for recovering the anchor from below the hawse hole.

THE NINETEENTH CENTURY

During the nineteenth century great developments were made in ship design and the ancillary equipment supplied to ships was improved. The seventeenth-century long-shank type of anchor and the later Admiralty pattern anchor both had the stock at right angles to the shank. This led to problems when these anchors had to be recovered. The anchor had first to be *catted,* or lifted by means of a tackle, to the short beam or *cathead* which projected from the bow. It was then *fished* by a tackle on the *fish davit.* Originally this was a beam that projected over the ship's bow abaft the cathead. Later the fish davit was changed to the radial davit and then to a gallows type davit.

However, the operation was still cumbersome and it was suggested by Hawkins in 1821 that his patent anchor, which was stockless and could be stowed in a hawse pipe, would avoid the prob-lems of handling the stocked anchors, but Hawkins's anchor lacked stability and further developments were not encouraged. Fifty years were to elapse before a similar anchor met with general approbation.

THE RODGER AND ADMIRALTY PATTERN ANCHORS

The *pickaxe anchor* patented by Lieutenant William Rodger in 1831 was almost identical to the anchor used by the Veneti tribe, though of better manufacture. In 1832 Rodger patented his *small palm anchor,* which, with some improvement, remained in use until the twentieth century as a stream anchor.

The *Admiralty pattern anchor* is the type most readily recognised as a typical sailing vessel anchor. Developed in 1841 under the guidance of Admiral Sir William Parker, it had a wooden stock, later to be of wrought iron, and curved arms.

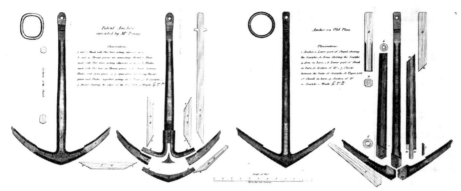

ABOVE: *Richard Pering's improved long-shank anchor (left) compared to the old pattern (right) in a 'Treatise on the Anchor' (1819). Pering's first test anchor was forged in 1813 and in 1815 the Navy Board adopted it for use in the Royal Navy.*

BELOW: *Commander William Rodger's improved patent small-palmed anchor, c1832.*

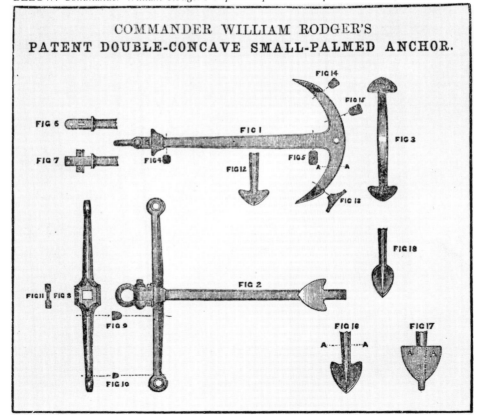

ABOVE: *Fishing a Rodger's improved bower anchor aboard the barque 'Pommern' in 1903. The fish tackle is attached to the gravity band on the anchor shank.*

RIGHT: *Types of anchor stock, from 'A Treatise on Ships' Anchors' by George Cotsell (1856).*

The Admiralty pattern anchor with its improved construction and superior quality iron represented the final development of the fixed arm anchor.

ANCHOR STOCKS

The iron stock was reintroduced at the end of the eighteenth century in small anchors and in larger anchors as the nineteenth century progressed. However, wooden stocks remained in use aboard vessels with timber hulls, the iron stock being mainly adopted in iron and steel hulled vessels. The Honiball, Porter and Trotman anchors were similar, differing only in the design of their palms and horns. The *Porter anchor* (1838) was developed to provide good holding with reduced weight, an advantage on merchant ships where small crews had to

Fig. 1. ADMIRALTY *Wood* Stock.

Fig. 2. Lieut. RODGER's *Wood* Stock.

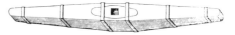

Fig. 3. ADMIRALTY *Iron* Stock.

Fig. 4. Lieut. RODGER's *Iron* Stock.

Fig. 5. COTSELL's *Iron* Stock.

21

An Admiralty pattern anchor from the royal yacht 'Victoria and Albert' (1899) at the National Maritime Museum. This type of anchor was introduced in 1841 by Admiral Sir William Parker. Its proportions of three to one were the same as those of the old long-shank anchor, so that if the arms are 4 feet long the shank is 12 feet. The centre of curvature of the arms is one third the distance up the shank from the crown. The iron of the anchor is elliptical in shape.

handle the anchors. This design was in three pieces, the crown, arms and fluke being a single piece that swivelled on the shank, to which it was attached by a belt; the stock was the first component.

Further developments were made to this design by Honiball in 1846 and Trotman in 1852. The *Trotman anchor* was widely used by merchant vessels, which often had one if not two bower anchors of this type. In the Royal Navy, where there was no shortage of manpower, they were not widely adopted and the Admiralty pattern anchor prevailed.

SINGLE FLUKE ANCHORS
For permanent river moorings the Admiralty pattern anchor was unsuitable,

as when the tide fell these anchors could penetrate a ship's underwater hull. To obviate this danger, some Admiralty pattern anchors had one arm bent over flush with the shank. Examples of this type of anchor have been recovered from the Medway and Pembroke dockyard. An example may be seen outside the Welsh Industrial and Maritime Museum at Cardiff. Generally, however, a single fluke anchor was forged and used for dockyard or river moorings. Anchors of this type had to be laid by boat or river service craft.

Navigational buoys and lightships require special types of anchor, and these may be of the screw, mushroom or clump types. Special craft are used to lay and recover these moorings, which usually

ABOVE: *The Porter anchor on the Anchor Wharf at the National Maritime Museum. This anchor was introduced in 1838 and was based on a similar anchor invented by a man called Piper in 1822.*

BELOW: *A Trotman anchor (1852) in the collection of the National Maritime Museum. The palms and horns are united, differentiating it from the Porter anchor. It was widely used on merchant ships.*

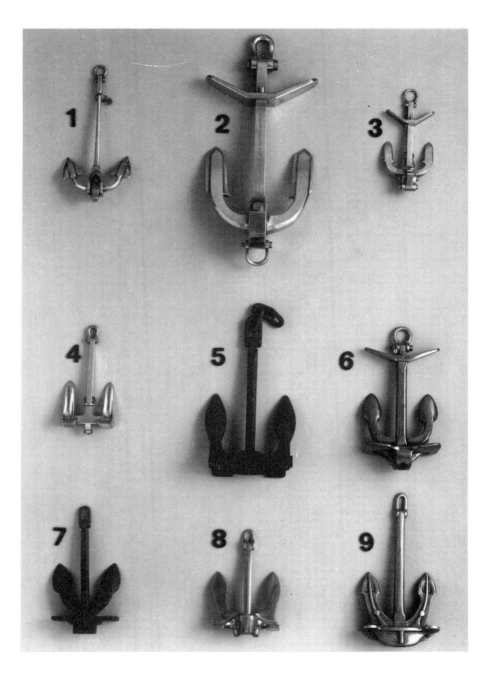

come under the care of a harbour authority, the Royal Navy or a lighthouse or pilotage authority such as Trinity House.

THE CLOSE STOWING ANCHOR

To enable the anchor to be stowed flush to the shipside or deck (in the latter case it was often placed on an angled ramp), the close stowing anchor was developed. To stabilise the anchor when digging in, a short stock in the same plane as the flukes was fitted to the upper part of the shank. The anchors of this type which were fitted in the early iron and steel hulled warships were a transitional development between the Admiralty pattern anchor and the close stowing stockless anchors which could be hove right into the hawse pipe or anchor pocket. The *Martin's anchor* of 1862, which was later improved, was widely adopted by the Royal Navy. In 1859 Francois Martin had demonstrated his anchor to the Brethren of Trinity House, Newcastle upon Tyne, and they recommended its adoption to shipowners and seamen on the north-east coast of England. Further trials were held by the Royal Navy at Woolwich dockyard prior to its approval by the Admiralty. Similar anchors were developed by Admiral Ingerfield, Lennox and Halle.

ANCHOR LEGISLATION

In an attempt to minimise the damage and loss of anchors and cables, proving houses, one controlled by Trinity House, were established to issue certificates concerning anchors and chain cable. The Chain Cable and Anchor Act (1864) regulated the proving and manufacture. Further amendments followed: that of 1874 required all anchors over 168 pounds (76.2 kg) to be tested and marked. In 1876 the Board of Trade issued instructions to surveyors that vessels under survey for passenger certificates should give satisfactory proof that their anchors of over 168 pounds had been tested in accordance with the Act. The most recent legislation has been the Anchor and Chain Cables Act (1967), operational since October 1970.

OPPOSITE: *A selection of model anchors.*
1. *Model of R. F. Hawkins's stockless anchor, patented in 1821. The shank terminates in a large eye, through which the forging which forms the two arms is passed.*
2. *The close stowing anchor patented by Francois Martin in 1859 was manufactured at Gateshead, Charlton Pier and Woolwich Dockyard. It was claimed to be the only anchor of the day without a weld, being made from forged sections. It was widely used by the Royal Navy before the advent of the stockless anchor. This model is of the improved Martin anchor, patented in 1872.*
3. *A close stowing anchor developed by Admiral Ingerfield in the 1860s. It differs from the Martin anchor in the way the head swivels on the shank, and in the tripping palm, which is triangular.*
4. *Wasteneys Smith's improved patent anchor, first patented in 1871, and subsequently modified. The shank is mallet-shaped, and the ends of the head form journals on which the arms are mounted and secured by pins.*
5. *Byers Admiralty pattern anchor is stockless, designed to stow with its shank inside the hawse pipe of a vessel, which is angled to take it correctly as the anchor is hove home. It was manufactured by W. L. Byers, Sunderland. The original design was patented in 1887; the model shown was approved by Lloyds Register of British and Foreign Shipping in 1904.*
6. *Persehouse Parks improved Hall's anchor was fitted with a short stock to improve its stability when digging in. This modification turned it from a stockless anchor to a close stowing type, and it was therefore unsuitable for merchant vessels with their smaller number of seamen. It was not widely adopted, though some naval vessels were equipped with it.*
7. *Taylor's patent Dreadnought anchor approved by Lloyds Register in 1909. Made of all forged parts, the two arms are separate and are kept in position by the head which passes over the end of the shank and the crown of the arms. A large cotter or locking pin holds the head assembly together.*
8. *The Baldt patent anchor was first approved by Lloyds Register in 1898. The company manufactured anchors in G. Hortshorne and Company's works at Dudley. The shank is inserted into the head through a hole on its underside, and the ball-shaped head of the shank is kept in place by a pin inserted through lugs on the head of the anchor.*
9. *Hall's latest improved stockless anchor, manufactured by N. Hingley and Sons, Netherton, near Dudley, and approved by Lloyds Register, 1910. Hall's was a Sheffield firm and their stockless anchor was first introduced in 1886. The head of the anchor was held on by a pin through the head, which in turn was held in position by keeps inserted in the head and secured by pins, or cotters.*

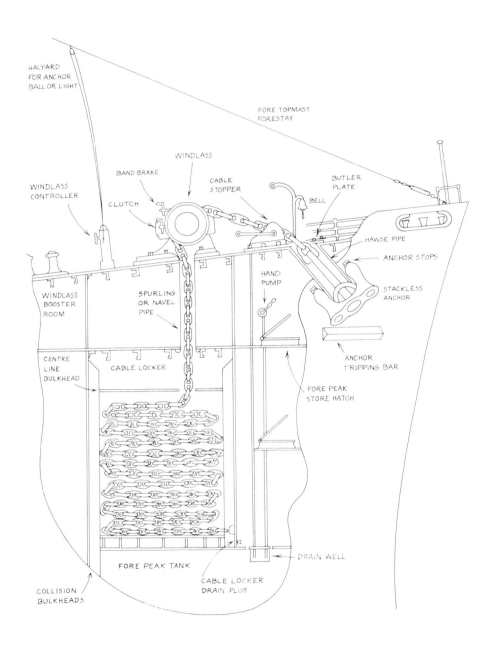

HALYARD
FOR ANCHOR
BALL OR LIGHT

FORE TOPMAST
FORESTAY

WINDLASS

WINDLASS
CONTROLLER

BAND BRAKE

CLUTCH

CABLE
STOPPER

BUTLER
PLATE

BELL

HAWSE PIPE

ANCHOR STOPS

STACKLESS
ANCHOR

WINDLASS
BOOSTER
ROOM

SPURLING
OR NAVEL
PIPE

HAND
PUMP

CENTRE
LINE
BULKHEAD

CABLE LOCKER

ANCHOR
TRIPPING BAR

FORE PEAK
STORE HATCH

FORE PEAK TANK

CABLE LOCKER
DRAIN PLUG

DRAIN WELL

COLLISION
BULKHEADS

Drawing of the ground tackle used on an 8000 ton general cargo ship.

26

Hall's improved stockless anchor at the Anchor Wharf at the National Maritime Museum.

MODERN DEVELOPMENTS

THE STOCKLESS ANCHOR

The requirement for an anchor that would stow easily into the hawse pipe of a ship, thus reducing the number of men in the anchor party on the fo'c'slehead, was met by the *Wasteneys Smith anchor,* patented in 1871. *Hall's patent stockless anchor,* developed by A. Verity and J. F. Hall and patented in 1886, became one of the most popular anchors of this type, though many patents for stockless anchors were taken out in the principal maritime countries. Examples are the Baldt anchor in the USA, 1898, the Brown Lennox in 1895, Byers in 1923, Samuel Taylor in 1892, the well known Dreadnought in 1909 and Canadian Steel Foundries' stockless anchor in 1908. Full details and sketches of the various anchors in the period 1890 to 1945 can be found in the book of approved anchor designs, published by Lloyds Register of Shipping in October 1945.

Stockless anchors are fitted with a large 'dee' shackle at the top of the shank to enable them to be attached to the plain link at the end of the studded link anchor cable. In the 1940s the lugless joining shackle for anchor cable came into general use. This shackle looks like a link of stud cable, but it comes apart after a steel locking pin is removed. As the joints in the shackle are machine finished, a special tool should be used to separate the parts and to avoid burring the edges of the joins.

The standard stockless anchor remained in favour with most merchant shipping companies until the 1960s, when high holding power anchors had proved their undoubted superior efficiency. However, some new ships are still equipped with anchors of the Hall or Dreadnought type.

THE TWENTIETH CENTURY

In 1943 a research programme into anchor design and efficiency at the British Admiralty Experimental Establishment at Haslar, Gosport, Hampshire, culminated in the production of the *Admiralty Cast (AC) 14 anchor* (1958). Supplied to new tonnage, this type of anchor was shown to have the holding power of approximately thirteen times the anchor weight (13W). A conventional anchor might only have the holding power 5W. Classification societies have

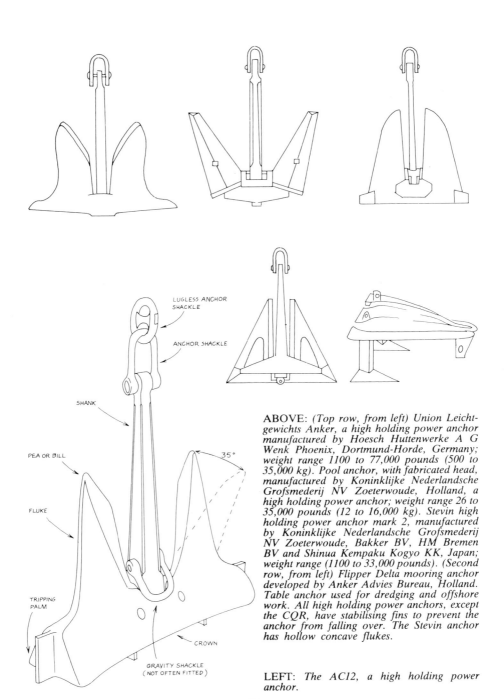

LUGLESS ANCHOR SHACKLE

ANCHOR SHACKLE

SHANK

PEA OR BILL

FLUKE

35°

TRIPPING PALM

CROWN

GRAVITY SHACKLE (NOT OFTEN FITTED)

ABOVE: *(Top row, from left) Union Leicht-gewichts Anker, a high holding power anchor manufactured by Hoesch Huttenwerke A G Wenk Phoenix, Dortmund-Horde, Germany; weight range 1100 to 77,000 pounds (500 to 35,000 kg). Pool anchor, with fabricated head, manufactured by Koninklijke Nederlandsche Grofsmederij NV Zoeterwoude, Holland, a high holding power anchor; weight range 26 to 35,000 pounds (12 to 16,000 kg). Stevin high holding power anchor mark 2, manufactured by Koninklijke Nederlandsche Grofsmederij NV Zoeterwoude, Bakker BV, HM Bremen BV and Shinua Kempaku Kogyo KK, Japan; weight range (1100 to 33,000 pounds). (Second row, from left) Flipper Delta mooring anchor developed by Anker Advies Bureau, Holland. Table anchor used for dredging and offshore work. All high holding power anchors, except the CQR, have stabilising fins to prevent the anchor from falling over. The Stevin anchor has hollow concave flukes.*

LEFT: *The AC12, a high holding power anchor.*

28

ABOVE: *The CQR anchor undergoing trials in 1933 in the West India Dock aboard the tug 'Westbourne'. The anchor weighed 3 hundredweight (152 kg).*

RIGHT: *The AC17 anchor, a high holding power bottom stowage anchor developed for use on nuclear submarines.*

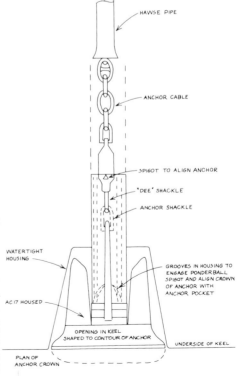

HAWSE PIPE

ANCHOR CABLE

SPIGOT TO ALIGN ANCHOR

'DEE' SHACKLE

ANCHOR SHACKLE

WATERTIGHT HOUSING

GROOVES IN HOUSING TO ENGAGE PONDERBALL SPIGOT AND ALIGN CROWN OF ANCHOR WITH ANCHOR POCKET

AC17 HOUSED

OPENING IN KEEL SHAPED TO CONTOUR OF ANCHOR

UNDERSIDE OF KEEL

PLAN OF ANCHOR CROWN

allowed a 25 per cent reduction in the weight rule for approved high holding power anchors. Admiralty experiments confirmed the importance of fluke area rather than weight in the holding power of an anchor, together with a sufficient length of cable.

The *CQR anchor* (1933), abbreviated from security patent anchor, was patented by Sir Geoffrey Ingram Taylor for use on flying boats, where anchors had to combine lightness with high holding power. It is a plough type anchor. It was widely used by power boats in both the Royal Navy and the Royal Air Force. Yachtsmen also found it useful and it was very popular with them in the late 1930s and immediate post-war period.

In the North Sea oilfields, semi-submersible platforms have been used since 1975 for drilling at even greater depths than was practised from mono-hulled drilling vessels. These new vessels were required to anchor in depths of 1200 to 3500 feet (360-800 m). In order to keep these platforms in position, a spread of eight or ten very high holding power anchors is used. It is not unusual to have anchors of 13.4 tonnes with 4000 feet

29

(1220 m) of 3 inch (76 mm) diameter special steel cable with a breaking strain of 1300 tonnes. Anchors are laid and recovered by anchor tender tugs.

HOW THE ANCHOR HOLDS

A long scope of cable ensures a horizontal pull on the anchor, enabling it to dig into the seabed. The catenary in the chain cable acts as a spring and restricts the pull on the anchor. If only a short scope of cable is paid out there is a danger that the anchor will break out of the ground and drag. The officer of the watch should take frequent anchor bearings of fixed objects if available, to ensure that the vessel is maintaining its correct position. These bearings, together with the ship's heading at the time they were taken, should be entered in the ship's logbook.

The anchor is marked by an anchor buoy on a grass or synthetic rope to ensure that it will be buoyant. This is attached to the wire anchor pendants. When the anchor is weighed the buoy and line are recovered by a four-pronged grapnel.

EMBEDMENT ANCHORS

For use in locations where vertical moorings are required the United States Army Material Command Engineering and Research and Development Laboratory has produced the *Seastaple anchor* that can be fired into the seabed. Embedment anchors can also have a vibrating head that drives the fluke assembly into the ground. The head may be recovered and reused.

DYNAMICAL POSITIONING

In recent years methods of holding a vessel in a selected spot by means of dynamical positioning have been introduced. Special or ducted propellers are fitted in each corner of the vessel, which can rotate through 360 degrees. These propeller units are controlled by a computer from a satellite navigation or radio position fixing system, or both. This type of ship positioning has been found most useful aboard certain types of craft used in oil exploration and well drilling and aboard diving service vessels. However, despite these developments, there will always remain a requirement in ships of the future for anchors of the high holding power type as well as for smaller anchors for yachts and other pleasure craft.

Drawing to show how the anchor holds.

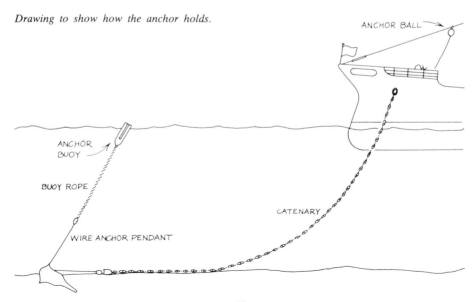

ABOVE: *Clump and mushroom anchors from the boom defence off Portsmouth.*

BELOW: *The MV 'Spey Bridge' (1969), 44,450 tonnes deadweight. The photograph shows the windlass and cable, and the spare bower anchor can be seen on the port side of the foremast.*

PLACES TO VISIT

Anchors or anchor models may be seen at these places. Intending visitors are advised to find out the dates and hours of opening before making a special journey.

HMS *Belfast,* Symons Wharf, Vine Lane, Tooley Street, London SE1 2JH. Telephone: 01-407 6434.
Bembridge Maritime Museum, Bembridge, Isle of Wight.
Cutty Sark Clipper Ship, King William Walk, Greenwich, London SE10 9BG. Telephone: 01-858 3445.
Dorset County Museum, High West Street, Dorchester, Dorset DT1 1XA. Telephone: Dorchester (0305) 62735.
Historic Ship Collection, East Basin, St Katharine's Dock, London E1 9LB. Telephone: 01-481 0043.
National Maritime Museum, Romney Road, Greenwich, London SE10 9NF. Telephone: 01-858 4422.
Royal Naval Museum and HMS *Victory,* HM Naval Base, Portsmouth, Hampshire PO1 3LR. Telephone: Portsmouth (0705) 822351 extension 23868/9.
Science Museum, Exhibition Road, South Kensington, London SW7 2DD. Telephone: 01-589 3456.
Welsh Industrial and Maritime Museum, Bute Street, Cardiff, South Glamorgan. Telephone: Cardiff (0222) 371805.
Whitby Museum, Pannett Park, Whitby, North Yorkshire YO21 1RE. Telephone: Whitby (0947) 2908.

FURTHER READING

Cotsell, George. *A Treatise on Ships' Anchors.* John Weale, 1856.
Bass, G. F. *History of Seafaring.* 1972.
De Karchove, Rene. *International Maritime Dictionary.* D. Van Nostrans Company Ltd, 1948.
Diderot, M. *Encyclopedie on Dictionnaire Raisonne des Sciences, des Arts et des Metiers.* Paris, 1757.
Frost, Honor. 'Egypt and Stone Anchors — Some Recent Discoveries'. *Mariners' Mirror,* volume 65, 1979.
Frost, Honor. 'From Rope to Chain — On the Development of Anchors in the Mediterranean'. *Mariners' Mirror,* volume 49, 1963.
Knight, Austin M. *Modern Seamanship.* Kegan Paul, Trench, Trubner and Company Ltd, 1905.
Martin, Colin J. M. *'La Trinidad Valencera:* An Armada Invasion Transport Lost off Donegal.' *International Journal of Nautical Archaeology and Underwater Exploration,* 1979.
Nares, Sir George. *Seamanship.* Griffin and Company, 1886.
Pering, Richard. *A Treatise on the Anchor.* Congdon and Hearle, 1819.
Saurwalt, K. J. *On the Holding Power of Ship's Anchors.* Krips Repro-Meppel, 1975.
Steel, David. *The Elements and Practice of Rigging and Seamanship,* volume 1. 1794.
Tinniswood, J. T. 'Anchors and Accessories 1340-1640'. *Mariners' Mirror,* volume 31, 1945.
Torr, Cecil. *Ancient Ships.* Argonaut Incorporated Publishers, Chicago, 1964.
Admiralty Manual of Seamanship volumes 1 and 2.
The International Journal of Nautical Archaeology and Underwater Exploration, volume 6 (1977) and volume 9 (1980).
List of Approved Anchors. Lloyds Register of Shipping, 1945. Supplement 1958. New edition 1977.
List of Manufacturers of Approved Anchors. Lloyds Register of Shipping, 1977.